D0066020

A GIFT FOR

Barbara

FROM

♡ Dawn

Each Day
A NEW
BEGINNING

Gentle Reminders to Love and Enjoy Today

LANCE WUBBELS

GIFT BOOKS

Each Day
A NEW BEGINNING

Copyright © 2011 Hallmark Licensing, Inc.

Published by Hallmark Gift Books,
a division of Hallmark Cards, Inc.,
Kansas City, MO 64141
Visit us on the Web at www.Hallmark.com.

All rights reserved. No part of this publication may be reproduced,
transmitted, or stored in any form or by any means without the prior
written permission of the publisher.

Editor: Jared Smith
Art Director: Kevin Swanson

This book in its entirety is an original creation of
Koechel Peterson & Associates, 2600 East 26th Street, Mpls, MN, 55406.
Original copyright © 2011 by Lance Wubbels.

Photography: unless noted, all photography © copyright ThinkStock.
Cover photo © ThinkStock.

ISBN: 978-1-59530-445-2
BOK4138

Printed and bound in China

TO KAREN

This is the day the Lord has made;

let us rejoice and be glad in it.

PSALMS 118:24

Many years ago, I was thrilled to receive an invitation to teach a class at a small Christian college near my home. Although I had deep aspirations to teach, I didn't think there was any chance I would get the job, since I didn't have any experience teaching at the college level. When the opportunity suddenly came, I went into overdrive in preparation, determined to make an impact on the students' lives by giving them the very best I could.

Two months into teaching the class, I was on a roll and getting excellent feedback from my students. I was so enthused I could hardly wait for the next lecture.

Then, without warning, at the beginning of a morning class, a young man made a foolish statement that I perceived to slight my teaching performance, which was followed by laughter from the rest of the class. Looking back, I realize I completely misread the situation. Nevertheless, the poisoned dart went straight into my heart, and I walked out of that classroom feeling crushed. A wave of depression settled over me like nothing I've ever experienced.

By evening, I was utterly convinced that the best thing for the students and for me was to quit. I spent the entire night alone, reading my Bible and praying, hoping for an answer, but with every hour my mood darkened. Even though I loved being a teacher and had given everything I had, I still wasn't good enough.

Around midnight, I was praying in my chair when my despairing heart was suddenly arrested. I am not a mystical person, but in an extraordinarily rare moment in my life, it was as though God spoke directly to my heart and asked:

> *Why do you need the students' approval? Who gave you the opportunity to teach: them or Me? If I am pleased with your teaching, what difference does it make whether the class is cheering or booing? It's not a popularity contest. Give Me your best and let Me take care of the results. Your joy is in Me, not in anyone else's applause. Tomorrow is a new day with a new beginning. Make the most of it.*

Instantly, the heavy gloom lifted, and the truth set me free. I went on to teach that course and other courses for another dozen or so years, and I loved and enjoyed every new day of it. Those were some of the most rewarding years I ever experienced.

Over the years that have followed, this same truth has helped me through similar challenges I've faced as a writer, a managing editor of a major publishing house, a husband, a father, and a friend. If I try to live my life based on what happened yesterday or what might happen in the future, I am doomed. Joy must be within me . . . every day . . . or I won't make it through.

Here's the good news: We don't have to experience life by constantly trying to repeat the past or anticipating the future. And we don't need to have a happy-go-lucky personality to love and enjoy our days. There are truths that truly can set us free in this life, and joy can become a daily reality that no person or circumstance can steal away.

EACH AND EVERY DAY

IS A NEW BEGINNING.

*Each and every day is a brand new journey,
and a bright future starts today.*

*Why wait another hour to start loving
and enjoying your life?*

Despite what we may have been taught to believe,

whether or not we love

       and enjoy this day…

       this very day…

       and every day…

    is really up to us, and the moment is *now.*

Give wings to your soul
by nourishing your mind.

If you can see the invisible,
you can do the impossible.

Have you ever asked yourself

why you sit waiting for the rain clouds

when you could be dancing in the sunshine?

RUN YOUR OWN RACE.

Live your life to win and never live to lose.

You're never too young

or too old

to dream new dreams.

100543535

POLAROID 32

Stay passionate

about seeing your dreams

come to pass.

100543534   POLAROID® 32

Remember that you are precious,

and your life is a precious gift.

Tell yourself that every day

is a gift from God,

for this is the absolute truth.

BE QUICK TO FORGIVE

and be kind and compassionate to others,

whether or not they deserve it.

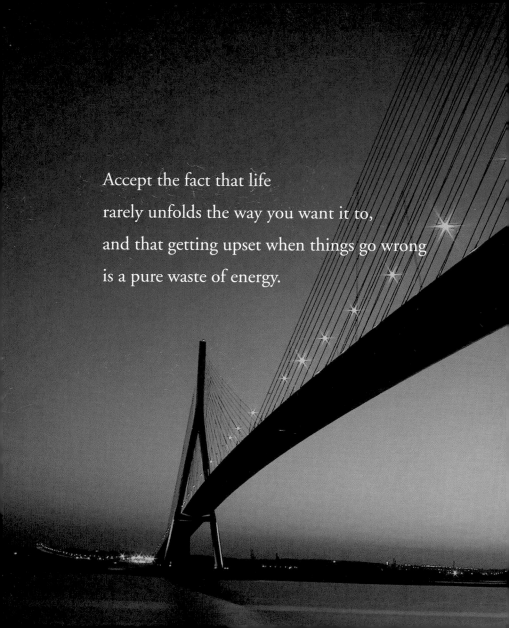

Accept the fact that life
rarely unfolds the way you want it to,
and that getting upset when things go wrong
is a pure waste of energy.

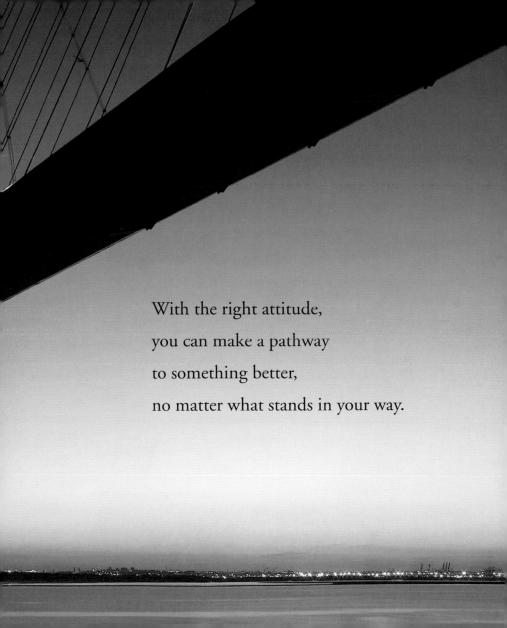

With the right attitude,

you can make a pathway

to something better,

no matter what stands in your way.

LAUGH EVERY CHANCE YOU GET.

It will keep you happy and healthy.

If the birds sing after a storm,

why shouldn't we?

If your sky is overcast today,

realize that the clouds will soon pass . . .

if you believe.

EXPLORE NEW PATHS

and have a burning desire

to learn new things.

Good ideas don't just happen.

They depend on people who are

open to making them happen.

JOY SPRINGS UP NATURALLY

when you find contentment
in what you have *right now*—

when you are truly grateful in your heart.

Life isn't measured
by the number of breaths we take,
but by the number of moments
that take our breath away.

When was the last time
your breath was taken away?

Be fearlessly free to be authentically you.
Refuse to play the game
    of acting out a life that isn't true
    to the person you are inside.
A lifetime of sincerity
    will reward you with riches
    far more valuable than silver and gold.

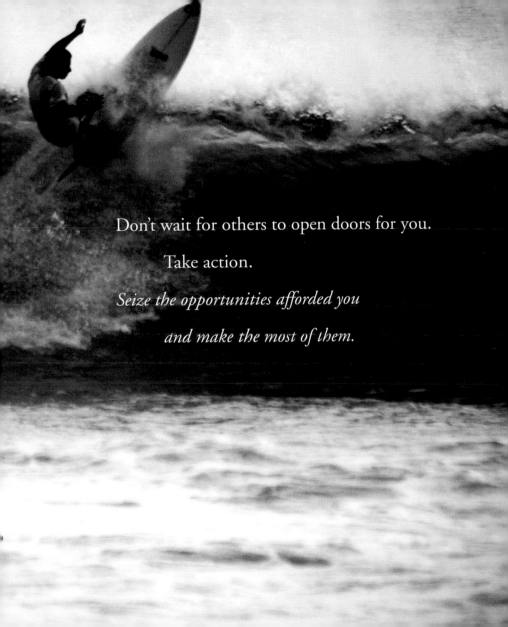

Don't wait for others to open doors for you.

Take action.

Seize the opportunities afforded you

and make the most of them.

If you can't see eye to eye with someone,

try to see heart to heart.

There's no law that says

you have to agree on everything.

King Solomon wrote,

"Buy the truth and do not sell it,"

 for truth is priceless.

May the thoughts you think

 and the words you speak

 always be true.

May your heart be free of deception,

 and may honesty

 be the hallmark of your life.

Sweet home

Find a reason to celebrate every single day.

See it for what it is:

a new beginning.

Follow your heart all the way to fulfillment.

You are unique in all of God's creation.

There has never been another you . . .

and there never will be.

You are filled with endless potential.

Today—whether this is the best

or worst of times,

or somewhere in between—

love others just the way they are.

Treat them as you wish to be treated.

REFUSE TO ACCEPT THE LIMITATIONS
and labels that have been placed upon you.
Be grateful for who you are,
and do not be faint of heart.
Be daring and wise.

Dreams come to pass when you step out
and take on the possibilities
that lie before you.

Do you chase after happiness

as if it is something you can buy

at a bargain sale or bottle

and hoard for yourself . . .

and then wonder why

you're missing out on the real joys of life

that are right in front of you?

Savor the moment.

Find something to love about

what you are doing *right now.*

BE GRATEFUL FOR EVERY GIFT

GOD HAS GIVEN YOU.

Your success or failure in life

will not be decided by the number

of setbacks you encounter,

but by how you react to them.

Use the storms of life to shape you

into a person of character and strength.

Never underestimate the power

of your own thinking.

Here's a simple life truth:

you become what you think about.

If you choose to think positive thoughts,

YOU'LL GET POSITIVE RESULTS.

WITH EVERY NEW DAY,

JOURNEY TOWARD TRUE HAPPINESS.

Take time for God, to read His Word,

to see His direction for your life.

Stand upon truth and never waver.

Go for your dreams and never give up!

Do something every day

   to make them come true.

Take up the challenge to do more and to be more.

Celebrate the sheer joy of being alive.

"Each man's life is but a breath,"

as the Bible says.

TAKE A DEEP BREATH

AND EXPERIENCE THE PRESENT MOMENT.

Savor the beauty and wonder of the world around you.

GUARD YOUR HEART,

for out of it flow the springs of your life.
Stay true to the values you cherish,
no matter what happens.

Life is too short to carry around

bitterness, grudges, and anger.

Don't waste your life in disappointment

or by trying to get revenge.

Your future waits to be written.

How foolish is it to allow what we

"hope will be one day"

to keep us from embracing today?

Start each day by choosing gratefulness and joy.

There is no substitute for an attitude
of genuine contentment.

DON'T BE AFRAID OF RISKS.

Fight through the fatigue

that stands between you and success.

Believe for the best to happen.

Hold the promise of new ideas

that can lead to a whole new life.

TAKE PLEASURE IN A SMILE.

Extend kindness to a neighbor.

Tell someone, "I love you."

"Man looks at the outward appearance but the Lord looks on the heart."

Embrace this ancient wisdom.

MAKE TIME FOR SOLITUDE—

to quiet your soul and ask

whether you are pursuing

your life's purpose.

Believe in the dreams and desires
God has placed in your heart.
Do not apologize for them.

Do everything you can to make them a reality.

As you make your way along your true path,

do not fear what others

may think or say about you.

DO NOT BELIEVE THAT YOU MIGHT FAIL.

You will succeed because you will not quit.

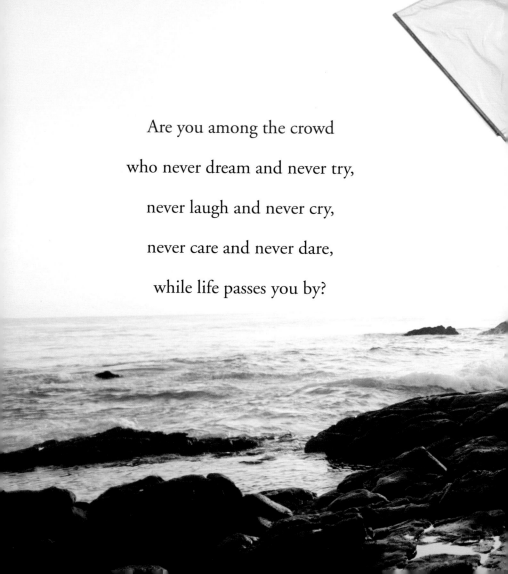

Are you among the crowd

who never dream and never try,

never laugh and never cry,

never care and never dare,

while life passes you by?

Live fully and joyously.

Dream about tomorrow,

treasure yesterday,

but live today.

This moment will not come again.

WHETHER OR NOT YOU UNDERSTAND
the challenges facing you
today or tomorrow,
understand that God is working through it
to prepare you for what lies ahead.

STAND TALL AND FACE
THE WINDS OF ADVERSITY.

LANCE WUBBELS is the vice president of literary development at Koechel Peterson & Associates, a Minneapolis-based design firm, and Bronze Bow Publishing. Before joining Koechel Peterson, he served for eighteen years as managing editor at Bethany House Publishers.

Wubbels has authored several fiction and nonfiction books, including the best-selling gift books with Hallmark, *If Only I Knew, Dance While You Can,* and *I Wish for You.* He has published three gift books with Inspired Faith, *Jesus, the Ultimate Gift, A Time for Prayer,* and *To a Child Love Is Spelled T-I-M-E,* which won a 2005 Gold Medallion award from the Evangelical Christian Publishers Association. His novel, *One Small Miracle,* won an Angel Award, and his 365-day devotional, *In His Presence,* also won a Gold Medallion award.

He and his wife make their home in Minnesota.

If you have enjoyed this book,

Hallmark would love to hear from you.

Please send comments to:

Book Feedback, Hallmark Cards, Inc.

2501 McGee Street, Mail Drop 215

Kansas City, MO 64108

Or e-mail us at:

booknotes@hallmark.com